How to Live Sideways
A Guide for Baháí Kids

by Michael Fitzgerald
Illustrated by John Burns

To Flannery

KALIMÁT PRESS
LOS ANGELES

O God!
Educate these children. These children are the plants of Thine orchard, the flowers of Thy meadow, the roses of Thy garden. Let Thy rain fall upon them; let the Sun of Reality shine upon them with Thy love. Let Thy breeze refresh them in order that they may be trained, grow and develop, and appear in the utmost beauty.

Thou art the Giver. Thou art the Compassionate.

—'Abdu'l-Bahá

Sing at the Feast... as loud as you can.

The Holy Spirit is the Bounty of God and the luminous rays which emanate from the Manifestations.

—'Abdu'l-Bahá

Invite the Holy Spirit over for dinner.

The earth is but one country, and mankind its citizens.

—Bahá'u'lláh

Stand up and hug the planet.

O well-beloved ones!
 The tabernacle of unity hath been raised; regard ye not one another as strangers. Ye are the fruits of one tree, and the leaves of one branch.

—Bahá'u'lláh

Have an extra-terrestrial over for a Holy Day.

O God, guide me, protect me, illumine the lamp of my heart and make me a brilliant star. Thou art the Mighty and the Powerful.

—'Abdu'l-Bahá

Pray upside down.

Táhirih was one of the first nineteen followers of the Báb. These first disciples were called the Letters of the Living. Táhirih was the only woman in that group.

At the conference at Badasht, in 1848, where many Bábís had come together to discuss the Báb's teachings, Táhirih created a sensation. Everyone in Iran, in those days, thought that women should always stay completely covered in public. But Táhirih threw aside her veil and showed her face in a gathering of men, proclaiming a New Day. This came as a shock to almost everyone. But Táhirih never wavered in her determination to fight for the rights of women.

Her name means: the Pure One.

Make up a song for Bahá'í girls to sing. Then, invite Táhirih to sing with you.

Nature is God's Will and is its expression in and through the contingent world. It is a dispensation of Providence ordained by the Ordainer, the All-Wise.

—Bahá'u'lláh

Earth Day has been celebrated on April 22, every year since 1970. It was established as a way of making everyone aware of the responsibility that we have to preserve and protect nature.

Climb a tree for Earth Day. Be a tree for Earth Day.

O Lord!

Make this youth radiant, and confer Thy bounty upon this poor creature. Bestow upon him knowledge, grant him added strength at the break of every morn and guard him within the shelter of Thy protection so that he may be freed from error, may devote himself to the service of Thy Cause, may guide the wayward, lead the hapless, free the captives and awaken the heedless, that all may be blessed with Thy remembrance and praise.

Thou art the Mighty and the Powerful.

—'Abdu'l-Bahá

Say your prayers by the light of the moon.

It is not for him to pride himself who loveth his own country, but rather for him who loveth the whole world.

—Bahá'u'lláh

Try Japanese food for International Peace Day. Try Persian food.... Try all kinds!

Of all the gifts of God the greatest is the gift of teaching.

—'Abdu'l-Bahá

Do some inexpensive travel teaching. Send a postcard to New Zealand.

Briefly, all effort put forth by man from the fullness of his heart is worship, if it is prompted by the highest motives and the will to do service to humanity.

—'Abdu'l-Bahá

Play ball to the glory of God.

E. G. Browne, who visited Bahá'u'lláh in the Holy Land, has reported that Bahá'u'lláh told him:

That all nations should become one in faith and all men as brothers; that the bonds of affection and unity between the sons of men should be strengthened; that diversity of religion should cease, and differences of race be annulled—what harm is there in this?... Yet so it shall be; these fruitless strifes, these ruinous wars shall pass away, and the 'Most Great Peace' shall come.

Dream big. Imagine the Most Great Peace.

Briefly, it is not only their fellow human beings that the beloved of God must treat with mercy and compassion, rather must they show forth the utmost loving-kindness to every living creature....

Train your children from their earliest days to be infinitely tender and loving to animals. If an animal be sick, let the children try to heal it; if it be hungry, let them feed it; if thirsty, let them quench its thirst; if weary, let them see that it rests.

—'Abdu'l-Bahá

Practice teaching the Faith to your pets.

The Greatest Holy Leaf was the sister of 'Abdu'l-Bahá, and the daughter of Bahá'u'lláh. She is known as "the outstanding heroine of the Bahá'í Dispensation." She wrote this prayer:

O Thou Kind Bestower, O Nourisher of our souls and hearts!

    We have no aim, except to walk Thy path; we have no wish, except to bring Thee joy. Our souls are united, and our hearts are welded, each to each. In offering Thee our thanks and praise, in following Thy ways and soaring in Thy skies, we are all one.

    We are helpless, stand Thou by us, and give us strength.

    Thou art the Protector, the Provider, the Kind.

—The Greatest Holy Leaf

Make a place for the Greatest Holy Leaf on your wall.
You can cut this picture out of the book.

As the hour of the attack approached for which [the shah's] army... was strenuously preparing, Quddús determined to sally out and scatter its forces.

Two hours after sunrise, he mounted his steed and, escorted by Mullá Husayn and three other of his companions, all of whom were riding beside him, marched out of the gate, followed by the entire company on foot behind them.

As soon as they had emerged, there pealed out the cry of "Yá Sáhibu'z-Zamán!" [O Lord of the Age!]—a cry that diffused consternation through the camp of the enemy. The roar which these lion-hearted followers of the Báb raised amidst the forest of Mázindarán dispersed the affrighted enemy that lay in ambush within its recesses. The glitter of their bared weapons dazzled their sight, and its menace was sufficient to stun and overpower them. They fled in disgraceful rout before their onrush, leaving all possessions behind them.

—Nabíl-i A`zam
From The Dawn-Breakers

Act out the Dawn-Breakers in the backyard.

They that have forsaken their country for the purpose of teaching Our Cause—these shall the Faithful Spirit strengthen through its power. A company of Our chosen angels shall go forth with them, as bidden by Him Who is the Almighty, the All Wise.

—Bahá'u'lláh

Be a pioneer. Travel in your mind.

War is destruction while universal peace is construction; war is death while peace is life; war is rapacity and bloodthirstiness while peace is beneficence and humaneness; war is an appurtenance of the world of nature while peace is of the foundation of the religion of God; war is darkness upon darkness while peace is heavenly light…

—'Abdu'l-Bahá

Pray for peace. Be peace.

O Son of Being!

Thy heart is My home; sanctify it for My descent.

—Bahá'u'lláh

Find your heart. See if you're in there. Use a flashlight, if necessary. Give your heart to God.

O Lord,

I have turned my face unto Thy kingdom of oneness and am immersed in the sea of Thy mercy. O Lord, enlighten my sight by beholding Thy lights in this dark night, and make me happy by the wine of Thy love in this wonderful age.

O Lord, make me hear Thy call, and open before my face the doors of Thy heaven, so that I may see the light of Thy glory and become attracted to Thy beauty.

Verily, Thou art the Giver, the Generous, the Merciful, the Forgiving.

—'Abdu'l-Bahá

Let 'Abdu'l-Bahá into your dreams.

Copyright © 1997 by Michael Fitzgerald

Cover and book design by Daniel Cook